TONIA BLEDSOE

Tech Equity: Leveraging AI to Bridge The Wealth Gap

Contents

Disclaimer

The information provided in this book is for general informational and educational purposes only. While every effort has been made to ensure the accuracy of the content, the author and publisher make no representations or warranties regarding the completeness, accuracy, or applicability of the information provided. The strategies, examples, and success stories shared in this book are intended to inspire and guide readers, but they do not guarantee specific results. Economic outcomes, including business growth, wealth creation, or other financial benefits, are subject to numerous variables, including individual efforts, market conditions, and unforeseen factors. The reader is encouraged to conduct their own research and seek professional advice where necessary.

Neither the author nor the publisher shall be held liable for any direct, indirect, incidental, or consequential damages arising from the use or reliance on the information provided in this book. Readers are solely responsible for the decisions they make based on the information shared. This book does not provide professional legal, financial, or business advice. Readers should consult qualified professionals before making any business, financial, or legal decisions.

Foreword

Today, I am thrilled to write this foreword for a book that aligns so perfectly with what I believe in, and it's written by someone I'm incredibly proud of—Tonia Bledsoe, one of the incredible participants in our AI certification program. "Tech Equity: Leveraging AI to Bridge the Wealth Gap" is a book that captures both the potential and the real-world impact of AI in a way that's inspiring, practical, and much needed. It's a roadmap to transformation, not just in technology but in opportunity, hope, and economic empowerment—particularly for Black communities facing systemic barriers for generations. Tonia has done a brilliant job of breaking down complex ideas into approachable, actionable steps. She's turning AI into an accessible tool for everyone ready to make a difference in their lives and communities.

When Tonia joined our AI certification program—she had a clear vision of what she wanted to do: use AI to empower others, bridge gaps, and bring tech equity to communities that have historically been left out of the conversation. And let me tell you, she is delivering on that vision tenfold. The stories she shares in this book, like those of Myra, Nehemiah, Sonya, Jennene, and Shauna, are not just case studies—they are real people whose lives have transformed because they embraced AI with courage, determination, and a sense of purpose.

This book is about the power of tools and, more importantly, the power of people—people who decide to take control of their futures, who leverage technology to solve real problems, and who create opportunities for themselves and those around them. The individuals you'll read about are doing that, using AI as their launchpad to succeed. Tonia writes with such warmth and clarity that you'll not only understand what's possible but feel motivated to start your journey with AI—whether that's launching a business, optimizing your day-to-day workflow, or taking a deep dive into an industry that you're passionate about.

I couldn't be prouder of Tonia and her work to pull together the insights in this book. It's not just about AI; it's about creating pathways to wealth, equity, and empowerment— and inviting all of us to be part of that movement. As you turn these pages, I hope you're as inspired as I am to not only dream big but take action. Because that's what this is all about: using technology to make dreams into reality, one bold step at a time. So, where do we start? Let's break it down: dive in, let these stories and strategies fuel your imagination, and then go out there and make some magic happen.

Tonia, thank you for your dedication and vision and for helping us all see how powerful we can be when we embrace the tools of tomorrow. Embracing AI for a brighter future!

Alicia Lyttle

Introduction: Taylor's Journey

Harnessing AI to Empower the Next Generation

At just 12 years old, Taylor dreamed of becoming an entrepreneur. When she learned about the Kidpreneur event in Washington, D.C., an opportunity for young business owners to showcase their products, she knew she wanted to participate. But with only three weeks to prepare, the odds seemed stacked against her—until she discovered the power of artificial intelligence (AI). Taylor's vision was clear, however. She wanted to create a line of all-natural skincare products because the harsh chemicals in store-bought items irritated her skin. She realized that many kids like her were looking for safe alternatives, and she believed she could fill that gap. But starting a business from scratch, especially with limited time, felt daunting. That's when Taylor turned to AI, specifically ChatGPT, to guide her through the process of starting her business in a very short time.

With AI as her partner, Taylor began her journey. She asked ChatGPT for safe skincare recipes, links to ingredients and containers, and even help with pricing her products. The AI tool provided her with ideas, suggestions, and resources, helping her refine her plans through multiple iterations. Taylor also anticipated the hot temperatures predicted for the day of the event, so she consulted ChatGPT on how to keep her products cool—ensuring that her lip balm, moisturizer, and face wash wouldn't melt in the heat.

But Taylor didn't stop there. She used AI-powered design tools like Canva to create product labels, develop QR codes, and build a landing page for her brand's online presence. In just three weeks, she had built a complete skincare line and crafted a professional brand identity. While her mom was available to review her work after long days at the office, Taylor was the driving force behind the launch, powered by the tools AI provided. By the time Taylor arrived at the Kidpreneur event, her brand was polished, her products were well-prepared, and she was ready to take on the world. The event was a tremendous success. Not only did Taylor gain confidence as a young business owner, but she also discovered the limitless potential of AI as a tool for turning dreams into reality.

The Power of AI: Closing the Gap

Taylor's story is more than just an inspiring tale of a young girl's entrepreneurial success. It's a glimpse into how AI can empower anyone—regardless of age, experience, or resources—to bring their ideas to life. In today's world, artificial intelligence is leveling the playing field, providing individuals with the tools they need to innovate, grow, and succeed. For African Americans and other marginalized communities, this presents a transformative opportunity to bridge economic gaps and create new pathways to success.

In the chapters that follow, we'll explore the powerful ways in which AI is being used to close the wealth gap, foster entrepreneurship, and empower individuals to overcome systemic barriers. Through real-life stories and practical insights, this book will demonstrate how AI can serve as a catalyst for economic empowerment, particularly within Black communities.

Welcome to "Tech Equity: Leveraging AI to Bridge the Wealth Gap."

Taylor's journey is just the beginning. As we move forward, you'll see how AI is helping people across different industries, ages, and backgrounds create opportunities that were once out of reach. Together, we'll explore the incredible potential of AI to drive equity, innovation, and economic prosperity for all.

Chapter 1: Understanding the Wealth Gap

So, what is the wealth gap, and why does it matter? Simply put, it's the economic disparity between Black and white Americans, a gap so wide that for every dollar held by a white family, the average Black family holds just fifteen cents. This gap isn't just about numbers—it's about opportunities lost and potential unrealized. But what if we could change that? Imagine a world where Black-owned businesses are thriving, where AI is leveling the playing field, and where communities once held back by systemic barriers are now flourishing. This vision isn't just a dream—it's within reach, but to get there, we need to understand the forces that created this gap in the first place.

After the Civil War, when slavery was officially abolished, the situation didn't improve significantly for African Americans. The Reconstruction era, which initially offered some hope for newly freed slaves, was quickly followed by the rise of Jim Crow laws. These laws enforced racial segregation and created new forms of economic oppression. African Americans were systematically excluded from wealth-building opportunities, such as land ownership and access to quality education.

Shawn Rochester, in his book "The Black Tax," estimates that the financial impact of racism on Black Americans has cost around $70 trillion since slavery began. Imagine the generational wealth that could have been built if African Americans had been afforded the same opportunities. Instead, this wealth gap has widened over time, contributing to a persistent cycle of poverty and economic inequality.

The Long Shadow of Segregation and Discrimination

During the era of segregation, Black communities were forced to live in separate, underfunded neighborhoods. Schools, hospitals, and other public services in these areas were vastly inferior to those in white neighborhoods. This created a cycle of poverty that was difficult to escape. One of the most damaging forms of discrimination during this period was redlining. Redlining was a practice where banks and insurance companies would literally draw red lines around neighborhoods where African Americans lived and refuse to offer them loans or insurance. This made it nearly impossible for Black families to buy homes, the primary means of building wealth in America. Even those who could afford homes were often denied loans or charged exorbitant interest rates. This lack of access to homeownership had a ripple effect across generations, as many African Americans were unable to build equity and pass wealth down to their children.

Civil Rights Movement and Economic Progress

The Civil Rights Movement of the 1960s brought about significant legal changes aimed at dismantling racial segregation and promoting equality. These changes marked a critical turning point for African Americans, paving the way for increased political and social rights. However, despite these legal advancements, economic disparities persisted. The Civil Rights Act of 1964 and the Voting Rights Act of 1965 were vital for securing legal rights for African Americans, but they did not address long-standing economic inequalities. Limited access to quality education, business opportunities, and generational wealth continued to impede progress in Black communities. Despite gaining political power, African Americans still faced major obstacles to economic equality, showing that legal rights alone couldn't close the wealth gap.

The Current State of the Wealth Gap: Statistics and Trends

Fast forward to today, and the wealth gap remains alarmingly wide. This staggering disparity is not just a statistic —it's a reflection of the enduring impact of historical injustices, compounded by modern-day challenges like mass incarceration, educational inequities, and limited access to capital.

Recent studies show that this gap is not only persisting but, in some cases, widening. For instance, a report from the Federal Reserve highlights that the median wealth of white households is nearly ten times that of Black households. This disparity is evident in every aspect of economic life, from homeownership rates to retirement savings. The COVID-19 pandemic further exposed and aggravated these inequalities, disproportionately affecting African American communities.

Job losses, reduced income, and lack of healthcare access have deepened the economic divide, making it even harder for Black families to achieve financial stability. Real-Life Impact: How Myra and Nehemiah Are Using AI to Level the Playing Field These systemic barriers aren't just historical relics—they continue to impact lives today, as seen in the experiences of individuals like Myra Hamilton and Nehemiah Thompson.

Myra's Story: Harnessing AI to Overcome Challenges

Myra Hamilton, a dedicated attorney with decades of experience, confronted a myriad of challenges as a solo practitioner. Despite her extensive knowledge in employment and labor law, Myra found herself grappling with the limitations of running a small, boutique law firm. The demands of managing client intake, conducting thorough legal research, and meeting tight deadlines often felt overwhelming. With no administrative support, she struggled to balance the operational aspects of her practice while delivering high-quality legal services to her clients.

However, Myra refused to be defined by these obstacles. Recognizing the transformative potential of technology, she turned to AI as a strategic ally. In July, she discovered AI tools that could streamline her workflow and enhance her productivity. By employing AI for document review and case summarization, Myra was able to significantly reduce the time spent on routine tasks, allowing her to focus on more complex legal matters. The integration of chatbots into her practice improved client communication, ensuring timely responses and efficient scheduling.

This innovative approach not only empowered Myra to manage her practice more effectively but also positioned her as a thought leader in the legal community. Today, she actively shares her insights on leveraging AI to close the wealth gap, inspiring other Black entrepreneurs to embrace technology as a means of overcoming systemic barriers. Myra's journey illustrates how embracing AI can transform challenges into opportunities, fostering growth and resilience in the face of adversity.

Nehemiah's Insight: Turning Adversity into Opportunity

Nehemiah Thompson, a business owner specializing in AI automation, faced significant challenges early in his career. He struggled with high operational costs and lacked access to lucrative projects. Despite his skills and unique services, breaking into markets dominated by larger, more established companies proved difficult. Nehemiah understood that recognizing these systemic barriers was essential for overcoming them. His turning point came when he discovered the potential of AI, not only as a tool for his clients but also as a means to transform his own business model. By leveraging AI tools like Canva and Gamma AI, Nehemiah automated content creation and streamlined operations, significantly reducing costs and enabling him to scale his services. This strategic shift allowed him to enter markets that were previously out of reach.

Through the integration of AI, Nehemiah was able to attract higher-paying clients and secure contracts worth up to $25,000. His story exemplifies how AI can empower Black entrepreneurs to overcome traditional obstacles to growth and achieve financial stability. Nehemiah's journey serves as a practical illustration of how small business owners can harness technology to scale their operations and compete effectively in broader markets. His experience highlights the importance of embracing innovation to drive business growth and address the wealth gap.

Why Understanding the Wealth Gap Matters

Understanding the wealth gap isn't just about looking at numbers and history; it's about recognizing the very real impact these disparities have on people's lives and livelihoods today. For business owners like Myra and Nehemiah, this understanding was crucial in navigating the challenges they faced and finding innovative solutions to overcome them. They exemplify how, by understanding the roots of these systemic issues, we can develop strategies to break free from their constraints and build a more equitable future.

Don't sit down and wait for the opportunities to come. Get up and make them.
*~ **C.J. Walker***

Chapter 2: The Role of AI in Closing the Wealth Gap

Introduction: AI as a Tool for Economic Empowerment

Artificial intelligence (AI) is more than just a technological innovation; it is a powerful tool that has the potential to transform industries and close the wealth gap for African Americans. In this chapter, we will explore how AI, particularly Generative AI, can be leveraged to create economic opportunities, drive business growth, and promote inclusivity within Black communities. As we delve into the potential of AI, we will also revisit the journeys of Myra Hamilton and Nehemiah Thompson, who have successfully harnessed AI to overcome challenges and achieve success in their respective fields. Their stories serve as real-life examples of how AI can be a catalyst for change, helping to bridge the economic disparities that have persisted for far too long.

Understanding the Wealth Gap: A Persistent Challenge

The wealth gap between African Americans and their white counterparts is a well-documented and deeply entrenched issue in the United States. This disparity is not just a matter of income differences; it is the result of centuries of systemic racism, discriminatory policies, and unequal access to opportunities. This long-standing disparity underscores the urgency of addressing the wealth gap and finding innovative solutions to close it.

The impact of the wealth gap extends beyond individual families—it affects entire communities. Limited access to quality education, healthcare, housing, and financial resources perpetuates a cycle of poverty and inequality that is difficult to break. However, AI presents a unique opportunity to disrupt this cycle and create pathways to economic empowerment.

Generative AI: A New Frontier in Economic Empowerment

Generative AI, a branch of artificial intelligence that enables computers to create new and original content, offers immense potential for addressing the wealth gap. By understanding and leveraging Generative AI, African American entrepreneurs and professionals can unlock new opportunities for innovation, entrepreneurship, and wealth creation. According to McKinsey, generative AI could add up to $4.4 trillion to the global economy annually. For Black communities, this represents an opportunity to harness AI for economic growth, job creation, and increased access to capital.

Innovation and Entrepreneurship

Generative AI empowers entrepreneurs to develop groundbreaking products and services, providing a competitive edge in the market. For example, AI can help create personalized customer experiences, streamline business operations, and develop new business models that cater to the unique needs of underserved communities. Access to Capital: Generative AI can also democratize access to capital by analyzing financial data, assessing risks, and predicting market trends. This can help African American entrepreneurs secure loans, attract investors, and grow their businesses in ways that were previously difficult due to systemic barriers.

Education and Workforce Development

Generative AI has the potential to revolutionize education by providing personalized learning experiences and upskilling opportunities for the future workforce. This is particularly important for African American communities, where educational disparities have contributed to the wealth gap. By leveraging AI in education, we can help bridge the skills gap and prepare the next generation for success in an AI-driven economy.

Myra's Journey with AI: Enhancing Legal Services

As we discussed in Chapter 1, Myra Hamilton faced significant challenges in managing her legal practice. The demands of her work left her with little time to focus on growing her business. However, by integrating AI tools like ChatGPT, Myra was able to streamline her workflow and improve client communication. By automating routine tasks, Myra not only increased her productivity but also provided more personalized and efficient services to her clients. This, in turn, allowed her to expand her practice and reach new levels of success.

Myra's experience highlights how AI can be used to overcome resource constraints and improve service delivery in professional fields, ultimately contributing to economic empowerment and closing the wealth gap. Myra's story exemplifies the broader potential of AI to enhance professional services.

Nehemiah's Path to Scaling His Business

Nehemiah Thompson's journey, also introduced in Chapter 1, illustrates the transformative power of AI in entrepreneurship. Faced with high operational costs and inefficiencies, Nehemiah turned to AI tools like Canva and Gamma AI to automate content creation and streamline his business operations. By adopting AI, Nehemiah was able to scale his business, attract higher-paying clients, and secure contracts worth up to $25,000. His success demonstrates how AI can help Black entrepreneurs overcome traditional barriers to growth and achieve financial stability.

Nehemiah's story serves as a practical example of how AI can empower small business owners to scale their operations and compete in larger markets. His journey underscores the importance of embracing technology to drive business growth and close the wealth gap.

The Broader Impact of AI on the Wealth Gap

The stories of Myra and Nehemiah are powerful examples of how AI can be a tool for economic empowerment. But their experiences are not isolated— they represent a broader trend of how AI is being used to address the wealth gap and create new opportunities for African Americans. Democratizing Opportunities: AI has the potential to democratize access to resources, capital, and opportunities that have historically been out of reach for Black communities. By leveraging AI, African American entrepreneurs can overcome systemic barriers, innovate in their industries, and build wealth that benefits not only their families but their communities as well.

Driving Economic Growth: As AI continues to evolve, its potential to drive economic growth in Black communities will only increase. By investing in AI education, training, and tools, we can ensure that African Americans are not just participants but leaders in the AI revolution. This will be critical in closing the wealth gap and creating a more equitable society.

The Path Forward

AI, and particularly Generative AI, holds immense promise for addressing the wealth gap and promoting economic empowerment within Black communities. Myra and Nehemiah's stories illustrate how AI can be leveraged to overcome challenges, enhance services, and scale businesses. As we move forward, it is essential to continue exploring and embracing the potential of AI to create new opportunities and build a more equitable future. In the next chapter, we will delve deeper into the practical strategies for integrating AI into Black-owned businesses, focusing on how technology can be used to drive growth, innovation, and inclusivity. The journey to closing the wealth gap is long, but with tools like AI, it is more achievable than ever before.

The power of technology can serve as a tool for liberation, creating spaces for innovation and entrepreneurship that were once inaccessible.
~ Kimberly Bryant, Founder of Black Girls Code

Chapter 3: Integrating AI into Black-Owned Businesses

Introduction: The Power of AI for Business Transformation

Artificial intelligence (AI) is not just a buzzword; it's a powerful tool that has the potential to revolutionize the way businesses operate. For entrepreneurs in the Black community, AI offers an unprecedented opportunity to innovate, scale, and compete on a level playing field. In this chapter, we explore practical strategies for integrating AI into these enterprises and how these technologies can drive growth, improve efficiency, and promote inclusivity.

As we dive into these strategies, we'll revisit the journeys of Myra Hamilton and Nehemiah Thompson, who have successfully integrated AI into their ventures. Their stories serve as practical examples of how AI can be leveraged to overcome challenges and achieve business success.

The Current Landscape: Challenges and Opportunities

Businesses led by African Americans face unique challenges, from limited access to capital and resources to systemic barriers that hinder growth. However, the rise of AI presents new opportunities to overcome these challenges. By adopting AI technologies, these entrepreneurs can streamline operations, improve decision-making, and create innovative products and services that cater to the needs of their communities.

Opportunities Presented by AI Automation: AI can automate routine tasks, freeing up time and resources that can be redirected toward strategic growth initiatives. Data-Driven Decisions: AI-powered analytics provide insights that help business owners make informed decisions, from market analysis to customer engagement strategies. Personalization: AI enables enterprises to offer personalized experiences to their customers, improving satisfaction and loyalty.

Myra's Journey: AI in Professional Services

Myra Hamilton's journey with AI offers valuable insights into how professional services can be enhanced through technology. As an attorney, Myra faced the challenge of managing a growing workload with limited resources. By integrating AI tools like ChatGPT into her practice, she was able to automate routine tasks such as document drafting and client communication.

How AI Transformed Myra's Practice:

Efficiency Gains: AI allowed Myra to handle a higher volume of work without sacrificing quality. She could draft legal documents more quickly and accurately, allowing her to take on more clients and cases.

Improved Client Communication

With AI managing routine inquiries and follow-ups, Myra had more time to focus on building deeper relationships with her clients. This personalized approach set her practice apart in a competitive market. Strategic Growth:

By freeing up time and resources, AI enabled Myra to focus on growing her practice, exploring new areas of law, and expanding her client base. Myra's experience illustrates how AI can be integrated into professional services to enhance efficiency, improve client satisfaction, and drive business growth.

Nehemiah's Strategy: Scaling with AI

Nehemiah Thompson's story highlights how AI can be used to scale a business, even in the face of operational challenges. As a solopreneur specializing in AI automation, Nehemiah needed to find ways to increase his capacity without significantly raising costs.

AI Tools that Powered Nehemiah's Growth:

Content Creation Automation: By using AI tools like Canva and Gamma AI, Nehemiah automated the creation of marketing materials, presentations, and other content. This not only saved time but also elevated the quality of his work, making it easier to attract high-value clients. Operational Efficiency: Tools like Fireflies helped Nehemiah automate meeting notes and follow-ups, ensuring that no detail was overlooked. This streamlined his operations and allowed him to handle more clients simultaneously.

Scalability: With AI handling much of the routine work, Nehemiah could scale his business without needing to hire additional staff. This scalability was crucial in enabling him to secure larger contracts and grow his revenue. Nehemiah's approach demonstrates how AI can be a game-changer for entrepreneurs looking to scale their businesses. By automating key processes, AI enables small business owners to expand their operations and compete with larger firms.

Strategies for Integrating AI into Your Business

If you're considering integrating AI into your business, there are several strategies to keep in mind. These strategies are designed to help you leverage AI effectively, regardless of the size or stage of your business.

1. Start Small and Scale Gradually: Begin with one or two AI tools that address specific challenges in your business. For example, if customer communication is a bottleneck, consider implementing an AI chatbot to handle routine inquiries. As you become more comfortable with AI, you can gradually expand its use across other areas of your business.

2. Focus on High-Impact Areas: Identify the areas of your business where AI can have the most significant impact. This could be anything from automating repetitive tasks to enhancing customer engagement. By focusing on high-impact areas, you can maximize the benefits of AI and see results more quickly.

3. Invest in AI Education: AI is a rapidly evolving field, and staying informed about the latest developments is crucial. Consider investing in AI education for yourself and your team. This could include online courses, workshops, or even consulting with AI experts to ensure you're leveraging the technology to its fullest potential.

4. Collaborate and Network: Don't go it alone. Collaborate with other businesses, join AI-focused networks, and seek out mentors who can guide you through the process of integrating AI. Networking with others who are also exploring AI can provide valuable insights and support.

5. Measure and Adjust: Once you've implemented AI tools, it's essential to measure their impact and make adjustments as needed. Use data analytics to track the effectiveness of AI in your business and be prepared to tweak your approach to achieve the best results.

The Broader Implications: AI as a Catalyst for Change

The integration of AI into Black-owned businesses is not just about improving efficiency or scaling operations—it's about driving broader economic empowerment. By adopting AI, Black entrepreneurs can create innovative solutions that address the unique needs of their communities, foster job creation, and contribute to closing the wealth gap.

Creating Inclusive Business Models: AI can help these businesses develop inclusive models that cater to underserved markets. By leveraging AI to understand customer needs and preferences, entrepreneurs can create products and services that resonate with their target audience.

Driving Economic Growth: The widespread adoption of AI within these enterprises has the potential to drive significant economic growth. As more businesses embrace AI, they can contribute to the overall economic health of their communities, creating jobs and generating wealth that benefits future generations.

Embracing the Future of Business

Integrating AI into Black-owned businesses is not just a trend —it's a critical step toward achieving long-term success and economic empowerment. Myra and Nehemiah's stories provide valuable lessons on how AI can overcome challenges, improve efficiency, and drive growth. By embracing AI, Black entrepreneurs can unlock new opportunities, compete globally, and close the wealth gap.

The future belongs to those who prepare for it today.
~ Malcolm X

Chapter 4: Leading the Way: Helping Your Organization Actually Adopt AI

I've lost count of how many times this has happened. A leader invites me in to talk to their team about AI. The room is full, the questions are good, and people are leaning in. And near the back stands the person who hired me, arms crossed, phone in hand, already halfway into the next meeting. They want their people to use this. They just have no intention of using it themselves.

I understand the instinct. When you are the one responsible for everything, learning a new tool can feel like one more thing you do not have room for. But I have to be honest with you, because this single detail, more than any budget or platform or rollout plan, is what decides whether AI ever takes root in an organization. Your team will adopt what you model, not what you assign. So before we talk about strategy or a company-wide rollout, we have to start with you.

"I Don't Have Time for One More Thing"

The first thing I hear, almost every single time, is some version of "we just don't have time to bring in another tool." And I believe it. Your calendar is full, your people are stretched, and the last thing that sounds appealing is a big implementation project on top of everything else.

So let me take the weight off that word. You do not "implement" AI the way you roll out a new payroll system. You do not need a committee, a six-month plan, or a line item before you begin. You start by using it. Once. On something small and real. The next time you have to write a hard email, draft a meeting agenda, or make sense of a messy spreadsheet, open the tool and let it help you with that one thing. That is the whole first step. It is not heavy. It is a fifteen-minute favor you do for yourself, and it is where every bit of momentum begins.

Start With Yourself, Not Your Team

Here is the shift I most want leaders to make. Stop thinking of AI as something you hand down to your staff, and start treating it as something you use yourself, as a partner in your own thinking.

When I sit with leaders, I ask them what they are wrestling with right now. A new pricing strategy. A tough hire. A market they are not sure whether to enter. And I show them that AI can be a sounding board for exactly those questions. Not to hand you the answer, but to think alongside you. You can lay out the strategy that is rattling around in your head and ask it to poke holes in it. You can ask it to play the skeptic, the customer, the board member. You can lean on it as a mentor when you are stuck, and as a thought partner late in the day when the office is empty and the decision is still yours to make.

That is the version of AI most leaders never see, because they only ever watch their team use it for tasks. But once you have felt it help you think through something that actually mattered to you, you stop seeing AI as software and start seeing it as a colleague. And that changes how you lead the entire conversation.

This idea isn't only mine. Around the time I started noticing this pattern, I read a book that put language to it, "The AI-Driven Leader" by Geoff Woods, and it stuck with me. His point is that most leaders shrink AI down to a faster assistant, something to clear emails and to-do lists, when its real power is to sharpen how you think. The shift he describes, from asking how do I solve this to how can AI help me solve this, is exactly the move I'm asking you to make. Used that way, AI stops being a chore you hand off and becomes a thinking partner you would not want to lead without.

Locking It Down Doesn't Work (People Just Hide It)

Now let's talk about the two reactions I see when leaders get nervous. The first is to lock it down. No AI, not yet, not until we figure it out. I understand the caution, especially around privacy and client information. But here is what actually happens when you ban it: your people use it anyway, and they hide it. I have watched this firsthand. Employees quietly lean on AI to get their work done, then stay quiet about it because they are not sure they are allowed to. Now you have the very risk you were worried about, with none of the visibility and none of the shared learning.

The answer is not prohibition. It is clarity. When you bring AI into the light, name what it is good for, and set plain guardrails around what should never go into it, you replace fear and hiding with something far safer: a team using AI out in the open, together, where you can actually guide it.

Decide How Your Company Will Use It, Then Say It Out Loud

Once you are using AI yourself and you have brought it into the open, the next job is to be clear about how you want your company to use it. Not vague permission. A real, stated expectation.

Some of the organizations I admire have gone as far as an "AI-first" posture, where the question on almost any task becomes "could AI help me with a first pass of this?" Others frame it as adding a new coworker to the team, one that never sleeps and is always ready to draft, summarize, or brainstorm. What I love about the ones who do this well is that they pair it with a human habit. They still meet. They still talk through what the AI produced, question it, and decide together what to keep. The tool does the first draft. The people do the judgment. That balance, clear expectations on one side and human review on the other, is what turns scattered individual use into an actual company capability.

And keep one eye on where this is heading, because it's moving fast. The AI most of us first met could only talk and draft. The newer wave, what people are calling agentic AI, can actually take action on your behalf, carrying a task from start to finish while you supervise, not just handing you words to copy and paste. You don't have to chase every new capability the moment it arrives. But notice what it means: as your AI coworker starts to do more than think out loud with you, the habit we just talked about, staying in the room and reviewing the work, matters more, not less.

Where a Leader Actually Starts

If you want somewhere concrete to begin this week, here is what I would do, in order. Pick one task on your own plate and do it with AI this week. Feel it before you preach it. Bring it into a real decision: the next time you are shaping a strategy, use AI as your sounding board and notice what it surfaces. Say the words out loud to your team: tell them AI is welcome here, name a way or two you want them to try it, and name what should never be put into it. Create one standing moment to share, a few minutes in a meeting you already hold, where someone shows one way AI saved them time. That is how it spreads. None of that requires a budget or a big launch. It requires a leader willing to go first.

The Tone Starts With You

Every organization I have watched adopt AI well had the same thing in common, and it was never the fanciest tools or the biggest budget. It was a leader who used it, talked about it, and made it safe to try. Your people are watching you to learn whether this is real or just another initiative that will pass. When they see you reaching for AI to think through your own hardest problems, they give themselves permission to do the same. You do not have to have it all figured out. You just have to go first.

You don't make progress by standing on the sidelines, whimpering and complaining. You make progress by implementing ideas.
~ Shirley Chisholm

Notes

Chapter 5: Revitalizing K-12 Education with AI: A Call to Action

The Urgent Need for Educational Transformation

The current educational framework, particularly in K-12, urgently needs transformation to match the evolving learning patterns, dwindling attention spans, and the distractions posed by social media. STEM education should lead the charge, preparing students to navigate and contribute to our increasingly technological society. As we observe global trends, countries like China and those in Europe are already incorporating AI into their educational curricula— a step we must also undertake to remain competitive.

For African American students, the integration of AI into education is not just a necessity but a crucial opportunity to close the wealth gap and ensure equal footing in a rapidly changing world. By embracing AI education, we can equip students with the skills necessary to thrive in a technology-driven future, fostering economic empowerment and breaking the cycle of poverty that has disproportionately affected Black communities for generations.

The Role of AI in Modern Education: Benefits and Challenges

AI offers a transformative potential for education by tailoring learning experiences to meet individual student needs, enhancing efficiency, and increasing accessibility. However, it also presents challenges, particularly concerning racial bias and the need for technology that is both inclusive and equitable.

Pros of AI in Education

Personalized Learning: AI can tailor educational content to individual learning styles and needs, significantly enhancing learning outcomes. Efficiency: AI tools can automate administrative tasks, allowing teachers to focus more on teaching and less on paperwork. Accessibility: AI provides educational opportunities to students in remote or underserved areas, promoting inclusivity and ensuring that no student is left behind.

Cons of AI in Education

Bias and Inequality: If not carefully designed, AI systems can perpetuate racial biases, adversely affecting grading and learning experiences for students of color. Lack of Emotional Intelligence: AI lacks the human touch, which is crucial for nurturing student-teacher relationships and understanding complex emotional and social contexts. Data Privacy Concerns: The use of AI in education raises issues around data security and privacy, with the potential for misuse of student information.

Mitigating Racial Bias: To counteract inherent biases, it's essential that AI in education is developed through a lens of racial equity. This requires intentional efforts from developers to understand and address potential biases in AI algorithms and datasets. Collaboration with diverse educators and communities in the AI development process can help ensure that educational tools are equitable and beneficial to all students. While AI offers transformative potential for education, its deployment must be handled with care to avoid reinforcing racial biases. By prioritizing the creation of unbiased AI tools and incorporating diverse perspectives, we can leverage technology to create a more equitable and inclusive educational landscape.

Sonya Hightower-Routt: Leading the Charge in AI-Enhanced Education

Sonya Hightower-Routt, a seasoned educator, recognized the urgent need for change in her classroom. Traditional teaching methods were no longer sufficient to meet the diverse needs of her students, who faced a wide range of learning challenges and distractions. Determined to provide the best possible education for her students, Sonya turned to AI.

How Sonya Integrated AI into Her Classroom

Personalized Lesson Plans: By leveraging AI-powered tools, Sonya developed personalized lesson plans that catered to the individual needs of each student. This approach ensured that all students received the attention and resources necessary to succeed. AI-Assisted Tutoring: Sonya implemented AI tutoring systems to offer additional support to students who needed help outside of class. These systems provided personalized assistance, helping students master difficult concepts and gain confidence in their abilities.

Administrative Efficiency: AI automation of routine tasks allowed Sonya to focus more on direct instruction and student engagement. This not only improved the overall learning environment but also enabled her to build stronger connections with her students and their families. Sonya's innovative use of AI in her classroom is a powerful example of how educators can lead the charge in transforming education. Her work has not only improved academic outcomes for her students but has also demonstrated the potential for AI to create more inclusive and effective learning environments.

The Imperative of AI Education for African American Students

Prioritizing AI education for African American students is crucial. The wealth disparity among African Americans remains a critical challenge, one that AI can help address by opening new pathways for economic advancement. By investing in AI education, we can equip students with the vital digital skills necessary for better employment prospects, increased earnings, and long-term financial stability.

Preparing Students for the Future

AI and STEM education must become central components of the K-12 curriculum to prepare African American students for the demands of the future workforce. This includes not only technical skills but also critical thinking, problem-solving, and creativity—skills that are essential in an AI-driven world.

Collaboration and Integration

Business owners, educators, and individuals must collaborate to implement AI education programs in schools. This can be achieved through partnerships with AI consulting firms, educational institutions, and community organizations. Integrating AI into existing curricula or creating dedicated AI courses will ensure that African American students are not left behind in the digital revolution.

Teacher Training and Access to Resources

To effectively teach AI concepts, educators themselves need professional development opportunities to enhance their knowledge of AI and its applications. Schools must also have access to the necessary AI tools, software, and hardware to provide hands-on learning experiences.

AI and the Future Workforce: Preparing for What's Ahead According to McKinsey, the integration of Generative AI and automation into the workforce is expected to significantly transform the job landscape by 2030. While this technological shift may displace certain jobs, it is also poised to create new opportunities, particularly in fields that leverage AI, such as AI system development, data analysis, cybersecurity, and specialized healthcare roles.

New Jobs and Skills

The future workforce will require a mix of technical and soft skills. African American students who receive AI education will be better positioned to pursue high-paying careers in fields that are shaping our future. The demand for professionals in AI ethics, privacy law, and AI system training is also expected to rise, offering additional opportunities for those with the right skills.

Economic Empowerment Through AI

Promoting AI education in schools can have a profound impact on closing the wealth gap for African Americans. By equipping students with AI skills, we empower them to pursue careers that offer financial stability and growth. Furthermore, AI consulting for Black-owned businesses can help these enterprises leverage AI technologies to improve efficiency, reduce costs, and enhance competitiveness, leading to economic empowerment, job creation, and wealth accumulation within African American communities.

Embracing AI for a Brighter Future

The imperative for AI education is undeniable. For African American business owners, educators, and the community, embracing AI is key to bridging the wealth gap and securing a flourishing future. By promoting AI education in schools and ensuring that African American students have access to the resources and opportunities they need, we can create a more inclusive and thriving society for all.

> "Enter to learn; depart to serve."
> **~ Mary McLeod Bethune**

Notes

Chapter 6: Building Skills for Tomorrow: AI Training and Lifelong Learning for Economic Empowerment

The Importance of Continuous Learning in the AI Era

As artificial intelligence (AI) continues to shape every aspect of our lives, the professional landscape is changing rapidly. For professionals within the Black community, this shift brings both challenges and opportunities. On one hand, AI could potentially displace certain jobs and deepen existing inequalities. On the other hand, it presents a unique chance to develop new skills, advance careers, and drive economic empowerment. In this chapter, we explore how AI training and lifelong learning can serve as powerful tools for navigating and thriving in an increasingly AI-driven world.

For African American students, the integration of AI into education is not just a necessity but a crucial opportunity to close the wealth gap and ensure equal footing in a rapidly changing world. By embracing AI education, we can equip students with the skills necessary to thrive in a technology-driven future, fostering economic empowerment and breaking the cycle of poverty that has disproportionately affected Black communities for generations.

Why Continuous Learning Matters

Technology is evolving faster than ever. Skills that were in high demand just a few years ago may soon become outdated, replaced by the need for expertise in AI, machine learning, data science, and other emerging fields. For those historically underrepresented in tech-driven industries, embracing continuous learning is crucial. Lifelong learning isn't just about keeping up; it's about positioning oneself at the forefront of innovation, where new opportunities for leadership and entrepreneurship abound.

The Changing Workforce: Opportunities and Challenges

The integration of AI into the workforce is reshaping the job market, creating both exciting opportunities and significant challenges.

Opportunities

New Career Paths: AI is opening up entirely new career paths that didn't exist a decade ago, such as AI system developers, robotics process automation, and ethical hackers and bug bounty hunters. For professionals from marginalized communities, these fields offer a chance to break into high-paying, future-oriented careers that are in demand across various industries. Higher Earning Potential: Acquiring AI-related skills can significantly boost earning potential. As businesses increasingly rely on AI to drive innovation and efficiency, those with the expertise to manage and develop AI systems are likely to command premium salaries. This can be a game-changer for individuals seeking financial stability and the ability to build generational wealth.

Entrepreneurial Innovation: AI is a powerful tool for entrepreneurs. It can streamline operations, optimize customer engagement, and unlock new markets. By leveraging AI, business owners can innovate in ways that were previously unimaginable, creating products and services that meet the unique needs of their communities and beyond.

Challenges

Job Displacement: While AI creates new opportunities, it also poses the risk of displacing existing jobs, particularly those that involve routine, manual tasks. People from underrepresented groups, who are often disproportionately represented in these roles, could face significant disruptions unless proactive measures are taken to retrain and reskill the workforce. Skills Gap: The rapid pace of AI adoption has led to a growing skills gap, where the demand for AI-related expertise far outstrips the supply. For those with less access to advanced education and training resources, this gap represents a significant barrier to entry into the most lucrative and secure jobs of the future.

Barriers to Access: Access to quality AI training and education remains uneven, with many communities lacking the resources and infrastructure needed to engage fully with these opportunities. This disparity can perpetuate existing inequalities, making it crucial to address these barriers head-on.

Practical Steps for AI Training and Professional Development

To seize the opportunities and mitigate the challenges presented by AI, professionals must take proactive steps in their professional development. Here's how to start:

1. Identify Relevant Skills:

Technical Skills – Focus on acquiring technical expertise in areas such as virtual/augmented reality (VR/AR) developers, data science, AI ethics, and cybersecurity. These skills are in high demand and will continue to be critical as AI technologies evolve.

Soft Skills: In addition to technical knowledge, developing soft skills like critical thinking, creativity, problem-solving, and adaptability is essential. These skills complement AI by enabling professionals to apply technology in innovative and socially responsible ways.

2. Leverage Online Learning Platforms:

Coursera, Udacity, edX, and even YouTube - These platforms offer a wide range of AI courses, catering to different levels of experience, from beginners just starting out to advanced professionals looking to deepen their expertise. YouTube in particular has become a genuinely solid place to learn, with entire channels dedicated to walking through AI tools step by step, for free. These courses are often flexible and can be completed at your own pace, making them accessible even to those with busy schedules. Specialized AI Programs: Look for programs specifically designed to help professionals transition into AI-related roles. These might include boot camps, certification programs, and degree courses that provide in-depth knowledge and practical experience in AI technologies.

3. Seek Out Mentorship and Networking Opportunities:

Mentorship - Finding a mentor who is experienced in AI can be invaluable. A mentor can provide guidance on navigating the complexities of AI technologies, offer career advice, and help you build a professional network. This can be particularly beneficial for those looking to break into fields where they have been historically underrepresented. Networking: Building a network within the AI community is crucial. Join AI-focused professional organizations, attend industry conferences, and participate in online forums and discussion groups. Networking can lead to collaborative opportunities, job offers, and the exchange of ideas that drive innovation.

4. Access Financial Resources:

Scholarships and Grants - Explore financial aid options specifically aimed at individuals pursuing AI education. Many organizations offer scholarships and grants to help offset the cost of training programs, making AI education more accessible to those who might otherwise be unable to afford it. Employer-Sponsored Training: Check if your employer offers reimbursement for AI courses or certifications. Many companies are willing to invest in their employees' professional development, especially in areas as crucial as AI.

5. Engage in Lifelong Learning:

Continuous Education - The world of AI is constantly evolving, and what is cutting-edge today might be outdated tomorrow. Stay updated with the latest AI trends and advancements by regularly attending workshops, webinars, and online courses. Lifelong learning ensures that you remain at the forefront of your field. Professional Development: Regularly seek out training sessions that allow you to apply AI in your current role. Hands-on experience is often the best way to deepen your understanding and build practical skills.

Shauna Adams: Revolutionizing Business with AI

Shauna Adams, a part-time business owner and operator of a travel agency, was struggling to keep up with the demands of running her business while managing her other responsibilities. The time-consuming task of maintaining a consistent social media presence was particularly challenging, leaving her feeling overwhelmed and stuck. Determined to find a solution, Shauna turned to AI.

How Shauna Integrated AI into Her Business

Social Media Automation: Shauna started using AI-powered tools to automate her social media posts, ensuring a consistent online presence without the need for constant manual input. This not only saved her time but also improved the reach and effectiveness of her marketing efforts.

Enhanced Customer Communication

By implementing AI chatbots, Shauna was able to provide instant responses to customer inquiries, improving customer satisfaction and freeing up her time to focus on other aspects of her business. Data-Driven Marketing: Shauna utilized AI analytics to better understand her customers' preferences and behaviors, allowing her to tailor her marketing strategies more effectively. This resulted in higher engagement and increased sales.

The Impact of AI on Shauna's Business

Increased Efficiency: With AI handling routine tasks, Shauna was able to operate her business more efficiently, leading to significant time savings and reduced stress.

Scalability: The automation of key processes allowed Shauna to scale her business without the need for additional staff, enabling her to take on more clients and expand her offerings.

Business Growth: As a result of these AI-driven improvements, Shauna's business experienced substantial growth, positioning her as a leader in her industry and a role model for other entrepreneurs.

Shauna Adams' journey demonstrates the transformative power of AI for small businesses. By embracing technology, she was able to overcome challenges, achieve growth, and create new opportunities for herself and her community.

The Impact of AI on Economic Empowerment

AI training and lifelong learning are essential not only for career advancement but also for broader economic empowerment within the Black community.

Pros of AI in Economic Empowerment:

Increased Job Opportunities: As AI-driven roles expand, professionals equipped with AI skills will have access to a wider range of job opportunities, many of which are well-compensated and offer significant growth potential. Entrepreneurial Growth: AI enables entrepreneurs to innovate and scale their businesses more efficiently. By integrating AI into their operations, businesses can improve productivity, enhance customer experiences, and access new markets, driving economic empowerment across communities.

Community Impact: As more individuals gain AI skills and start successful businesses, the economic upliftment of entire communities can accelerate. This collective progress contributes to closing the wealth gap and creating a more equitable society.

Cons of AI in Economic Empowerment

Access Barriers: The uneven distribution of AI education and training opportunities can exacerbate existing inequalities. Without targeted efforts to provide access to underrepresented communities, AI could reinforce rather than reduce economic disparities.

Potential Bias: If not carefully designed and implemented, AI systems can perpetuate biases that disadvantage underrepresented groups. This underscores the importance of inclusive AI development practices that actively seek to minimize and eliminate bias.

Economic Displacement: The rapid pace of AI adoption may outpace the ability of workers to retrain and reskill, particularly in communities that lack robust support systems for workforce development. This could lead to increased unemployment and underemployment if not addressed.

Empowering the Future Workforce

In today's rapidly evolving economy, AI training and lifelong learning are not just valuable they are essential for professionals to thrive. By embracing these opportunities, individuals can secure their place in the future workforce, drive economic empowerment, and contribute to closing the wealth gap. The journey toward economic empowerment begins with a commitment to continuous education and professional growth in the AI era. Shauna's story is a powerful testament to the impact of embracing a growth mindset and the importance of community. Not only did she equip herself with the latest AI tools, but she also surrounded herself with a strong network of fellow AI consultants. This community became a source of inspiration, support, and collaboration. Shauna leaned on her peers when facing challenges, never hesitating to seek guidance. At the same time, she eagerly offered her insights and assistance, embodying the reciprocal nature of true professional networks.

As AI continues to transform industries and redefine the job market, those who are prepared with the right skills, a willingness to learn, and a supportive community will not only participate in the AI revolution but lead it. Shauna's journey illustrates that thriving in this new landscape requires more than just technical skills; it demands an openness to growth, a commitment to lifelong learning, and the ability to both give and receive support within a community of like-minded professionals.

By investing in AI training, fostering a culture of continuous learning, and building strong networks, professionals can ensure that they are at the forefront of this transformation. Together, these efforts will create a future that is more inclusive, equitable, and prosperous for all, where individuals like Shauna not only succeed but help others rise with them.

You have to wake up each day believing you can make a difference, and that every step you take can lead to something greater.
~ Oprah Winfrey

Notes

Chapter 7: Building Partnerships for Success

The Power of Collaboration in AI

In today's fast-paced world, artificial intelligence (AI) is revolutionizing industries and shaping the future. However, many African American business owners, educators, and individuals have yet to fully tap into AI's potential. This is often due to the complexities of AI and the barriers to access that exist within the community. But there's a powerful way to overcome these challenges: by building strategic partnerships. By collaborating with AI consulting firms, educational institutions, and community organizations, Black entrepreneurs and professionals can gain the expertise, resources, and networks needed to fully integrate AI into their businesses, schools, and personal development. These partnerships are not just about adopting technology; they're about driving economic empowerment and closing the wealth gap.

Collaborating with AI Consulting Firms

One of the best ways to navigate the complexities of AI is by partnering with AI consulting firms. These firms specialize in guiding businesses through the intricacies of AI, offering customized solutions that align with specific goals. For African American entrepreneurs and professionals, such partnerships can be transformative.

Key Benefits of Partnering with AI Consulting Firms

Expertise Access: AI consulting firms bring a wealth of knowledge and experience. They stay ahead of the latest trends and best practices, which is invaluable for business owners who might not have in-house AI specialists. Tailored Services: Every business is unique, and AI consulting firms excel at creating solutions that cater to specific needs. Whether it's strategy development, data analysis, or process automation, these firms can tailor their services to address the challenges faced by Black-owned businesses.

Networking Opportunities

Partnering with an AI consulting firm can also open doors to a broader network of industry partners, investors, and resources. These connections are crucial for scaling a business, securing funding, and accessing new markets.

Case Study: Nehemiah Thompson's Joint Venture Success

Nehemiah Thompson, an entrepreneur with a knack for backend automations, realized that while he excelled at optimizing AI-driven processes, he wasn't passionate about creating content. Instead of struggling through the aspects of business he didn't enjoy, Nehemiah decided to find a partner whose strengths complemented his own. He entered into a joint venture with someone who loved content creation but wasn't as comfortable with the technical side of automation.

This partnership turned out to be a perfect match, like peanut butter and jelly. With each partner focusing on what they do best, their business began to thrive.

Nehemiah handled the backend automations, ensuring that operations ran smoothly and efficiently, while his partner took charge of creating engaging content that resonated with their audience. The synergy between their skills made scaling the business easy, as they could each dedicate their time and energy to their areas of strength.

Nehemiah's experience highlights the power of partnerships in business. By finding a partner whose skills complemented his own, he was able to grow his business more effectively and enjoy the work he does every day.

Partnering with Educational Institutions

Educational institutions play a vital role in preparing the next generation of AI professionals and ensuring that Black students are equipped with the skills needed to thrive in a tech-driven economy. By partnering with schools, colleges, and universities, businesses can help shape curricula that meet the demands of the AI workforce while also benefiting from a pipeline of talented, well-prepared graduates.

Key Benefits of Partnering with Educational Institutions

Talent Pipeline: Collaborating with educational institutions allows businesses to establish internships, apprenticeships, and mentorship programs that provide students with hands-on experience in AI. This not only helps students develop practical skills but also creates a talent pipeline for businesses looking to hire AI-savvy employees.

Curriculum Enhancement: Businesses can work with educators to enhance curricula, ensuring that the skills being taught align with the current and future needs of the job market. This collaboration can lead to the development of specialized programs in AI, data science, and related fields, tailored to prepare Black students for success in these areas.

Access to AI Solutions: Educational institutions often collaborate with tech programs and research initiatives focused on developing cutting-edge AI applications. By partnering with these institutions, businesses can gain access to innovative AI solutions and research that can be applied to their operations.

Engaging with Community Organizations

Community organizations are essential allies in promoting economic empowerment and closing the wealth gap. These organizations understand the unique challenges faced by African Americans and often lead the way in advocating for systemic change. By engaging with community organizations, businesses and individuals can build strong networks, foster collaboration, and drive meaningful impact.

Key Benefits of Engaging with Community Organizations:

Community Networks: Community organizations provide a platform for businesses to connect with like-minded individuals and groups that share a commitment to economic empowerment. These networks can lead to valuable collaborations, partnerships, and support systems that benefit everyone involved.

Educational Program Development: Many community organizations develop and deliver educational programs tailored to the needs of Black students and professionals. By partnering with these organizations, businesses can contribute to these initiatives, helping to shape programs that provide AI training, financial literacy, and entrepreneurship education.

Advocacy and Policy Influence: Community organizations play a critical role in advocating for policies that promote economic equality and address systemic barriers. By working with these organizations, businesses can support advocacy efforts that push for greater access to AI education, funding, and resources for Black communities.

Networking and Mentorship Opportunities

Networking and mentorship are essential for professional growth, especially in the rapidly evolving field of AI. For Black professionals, having access to mentors and networks within the AI industry can make a significant difference in overcoming career challenges and advancing in their fields.

Key Benefits of Networking and Mentorship

Professional Growth: Expanding one's network within the AI community opens up opportunities for collaboration, knowledge sharing, and career advancement. Networking events, conferences, and online forums are great places to connect with peers, industry leaders, and potential collaborators. Guidance and Support: Mentorship provides invaluable guidance for professionals at all stages of their careers. Experienced mentors can offer insights into the AI industry, help navigate challenges, and provide support as mentees work toward their goals. For Black professionals in AI, mentorship can also help in overcoming barriers related to representation and inclusivity.

Industry Leadership: By actively participating in networking and mentorship opportunities, Black professionals can establish themselves as thought leaders within the AI industry. This not only enhances their careers but also contributes to diversifying leadership within the field.

Empowering Through Partnerships

Building partnerships is a powerful strategy for Black professionals and entrepreneurs to harness the full potential of AI and drive economic empowerment. Whether through collaborations with AI consulting firms, educational institutions, or community organizations, or by expanding networks and seeking mentorship, these partnerships provide the expertise, resources, and support needed to succeed in an increasingly AI-driven world. By embracing these strategies, African American stakeholders can close the wealth gap, enhance competitiveness, and foster educational and economic empowerment within their communities. The path to success in the AI era is paved with collaboration, and by working together, we can ensure a more inclusive and prosperous future for all.

"The best way to lift one's self up is to help someone else."
~ Booker T. Washington

Notes

Chapter 8: AI and Economic Empowerment: Bridging the Wealth Gap

The Promise of AI for Economic Equity

Artificial Intelligence (AI) is more than just a technological advancement; it is a powerful tool that holds the potential to transform economies and create a more equitable society. For African Americans, who have historically been marginalized in many aspects of economic life, AI presents both a challenge and an opportunity. By strategically adopting AI technologies, Black entrepreneurs and professionals can drive economic empowerment and help close the wealth gap that has persisted for generations.

In this chapter, we delve into how AI is being used to bridge the wealth gap and explore the real-life stories of individuals who have leveraged AI to create economic opportunities within their communities.

AI as a Tool for Economic Empowerment

The integration of AI into various sectors offers numerous opportunities for economic growth. However, these opportunities are often unequally distributed, with marginalized communities facing barriers to access. By intentionally embracing AI, Black professionals and entrepreneurs can overcome these barriers and harness AI's transformative power for economic gain.

Key Areas Where AI Can Drive Economic Empowerment

Entrepreneurial Growth: AI enables entrepreneurs to innovate and scale their businesses more efficiently. Through automation, data analysis, and personalized marketing, business owners can reach new markets, optimize operations, and increase profitability. Job Creation: AI has the potential to create new job opportunities in fields such as voice user interface (VUI) designers, data science, and bioinformatics specialists. By gaining expertise in these areas, individuals can secure high-paying jobs and contribute to the economic upliftment of their communities.

Financial Inclusion: AI-driven financial technologies (fintech) can provide underbanked and underserved communities with access to banking services, credit, and investment opportunities, helping to build wealth and financial stability.

Case Study: Jennene Biggins' AI-Driven Transformation and Economic Empowerment

Jennene Biggins, a solopreneur and founder of a text marketing company, sought to drive her business forward by overcoming a series of entrenched challenges that limited her growth. As a small business owner, she was handling multiple roles herself, from client acquisition and service delivery to content creation and client management. By embracing AI, Jennene was able to streamline operations, increase her productivity, and ultimately achieve measurable financial growth—all within a short time frame. Her journey highlights how AI can be a powerful enabler of economic empowerment for small business owners, transforming limitations into strategic advantages.

Challenges Jennene Faced

Jennene's journey began with several key challenges common to solopreneurs aiming to scale: Time and Resource Constraints: Managing her company's operations, marketing, and client communications left Jennene with little time for strategic growth. The repetitive nature of her daily tasks prevented her from focusing on high-level business development, restricting her ability to take on new clients and expand her services. Client Capacity and Engagement: As her business grew, Jennene encountered limitations in her ability to handle a larger client base while maintaining the same level of service quality. High demands on her time often meant delayed responses, reduced engagement, and missed opportunities to build stronger client relationships.

Need for Business Growth and Financial Stability

Jennene aimed to increase her income and establish a stable revenue stream, but her limited capacity to scale and manage new clients made financial growth challenging. Without a streamlined approach, her business's financial outlook remained limited by the hours she could personally devote to client work.

Jennene's challenges reflect the broader issues faced by many small business owners, where limited time and resources can hinder growth and reduce the business's ability to reach its full economic potential.

Solutions Jennene Implemented

Upon discovering the potential of AI to optimize business processes, Jennene embarked on a journey of transformation. Her approach to AI was not just about adopting tools but strategically integrating solutions that aligned with her goals for business growth and operational efficiency. The following solutions allowed Jennene to overcome her limitations: Text Marketing Automation: Jennene leveraged AI-driven chatbots and automated text marketing platforms, allowing her to automate customer interactions and outreach. These tools enabled her to respond to client inquiries instantly, nurture leads, and deliver consistent service, reducing the burden of constant manual engagement. As a result, she was able to provide personalized client interactions at scale, freeing up her time while enhancing customer satisfaction.

Intelligent Workflow Streamlining

AI-powered toolshelped Jennene automate her most repetitive tasks, including content creation, marketing, and scheduling. How? By automating aspects of her social media and marketing efforts, she maintained a consistent online presence with minimal effort. This allowed her to reallocate her time to high-impact tasks such as strategic planning and business development, accelerating her company's growth trajectory.

Enhanced Data-Driven Marketing

Through AI analytics, Jennene gained insights into client behavior, preferences, and engagement patterns. By understanding what resonated most with her audience, she could tailor her marketing campaigns, refine her content, and better target her services to meet client needs. This data-driven approach increased the effectiveness of her campaigns, converting more leads into paying clients.

Increased Scalability through Automation

By embracing AI tools, Jennene expanded her business capacity without the need for additional staff. With automated systems handling routine operations and client communications, she scaled her business sustainably, positioning her to serve more clients and accommodate growth with minimal overhead.

Outcomes Jennene Achieved

The adoption of AI produced transformative outcomes in Jennene's business, both financially and operationally: Significant Financial Growth: Within the first month of implementing AI solutions, Jennene secured a $35,000 project—a significant financial gain that underscored the tangible benefits of AI integration. This project marked a milestone in her business, demonstrating the scalability and financial potential made possible by AI.

Increased Productivity and Client Capacity

With AI managing repetitive tasks and enhancing client interactions, Jennene was able to focus her efforts on onboarding new clients and delivering high-value services. Her productivity rose significantly, allowing her to accommodate a larger client base and serve more clients without compromising on service quality.

Enhanced Client Relationships and Engagement

The automated communication tools Jennene implemented improved client response times and engagement, creating a more seamless customer experience. By automating routine follow-ups and personalized communications, she fostered stronger relationships with clients, leading to higher satisfaction and retention rates.

Economic Empowerment and Business Resilience

AI enabled Jennene to increase her income while establishing a sustainable business model that could withstand economic fluctuations. By reducing her dependency on manual processes, she created a resilient operation capable of adapting to changing demands. Her journey demonstrates how small business owners can leverage AI to break through growth barriers, achieve financial stability, and contribute to economic empowerment within their communities. Jennene's success story highlights the broader impact of AI as a tool for economic empowerment. By transforming her business through AI, she was able to overcome systemic challenges faced by many solopreneurs, imited resources, constrained capacity, and financial instability. Her journey serves as a powerful example of how emerging technology can bridge gaps, drive business success, and empower small business owners to reach new heights.

Harnessing AI for Economic Empowerment

Jennene Biggins' journey embodies the transformative power of AI for solopreneurs and small business owners alike, showing how technology can help break through traditional growth barriers. Through her adoption of AI, Jennene didn't just improve productivity or profit—she built a sustainable, resilient business model capable of scaling with fewer resources, ultimately achieving a level of growth that had previously seemed out of reach. Her story is a powerful reminder of AI's potential to democratize access to opportunity, empowering individuals to take control of their economic futures. By embracing AI to streamline tasks, make data-driven decisions, and optimize client relationships, Jennene exemplifies how small businesses can harness technology to foster economic empowerment, not only for themselves but also for their communities.

The Path Forward

While AI offers immense potential for economic empowerment, the path forward is not without obstacles. Access to AI technologies, the skills gap, and systemic barriers continue to challenge many within the Black community. However, by adopting a proactive approach, these challenges can be met head-on.

Strategies for Overcoming Challenges

Investing in Education: Continuous learning and upskilling are critical in the AI era. By investing in education—both formal and informal—individuals can equip themselves with the skills needed to thrive in an AI-driven economy.

Building Strong Networks: Collaboration and community support are essential for overcoming barriers. By building strong networks, professionals and entrepreneurs can access the resources, mentorship, and opportunities needed to succeed.

Advocating for Inclusivity: Advocacy plays a crucial role in ensuring that AI technologies are developed and deployed in ways that are inclusive and equitable. By participating in advocacy efforts, individuals can help shape the policies and practices that govern AI's impact on society.

The Transformative Power of AI

The integration of AI into various sectors is not just a technological shift; it is a pathway to economic empowerment and social equity. By strategically adopting AI, Black professionals and entrepreneurs can overcome systemic barriers, drive innovation, and contribute to closing the wealth gap. The stories of individuals like Sonya Hightower-Routt, Nehemiah Thompson, Myra Hamilton, and Shauna Adams serve as powerful examples of how AI can be used to create lasting change within communities.

As we look to the future, it is clear that AI will continue to play a pivotal role in shaping the economic landscape. By embracing this technology and working together to overcome challenges, we can ensure that the benefits of AI are accessible to all, creating a more inclusive and prosperous future.

AI has the potential to be a tool for everyone, but we must ensure that it is accessible to everyone, and that means breaking down barriers to adoption and innovation.

~ Dr. Ayanna Howard

Chapter 9: Embracing the Future: A Call to Action

Here is the moment I think about most. Someone leaves one of my workshops lit up. They have pages of notes, a head full of ideas, and every intention of getting started. And then Monday comes. The inbox is full, the day gets away from them, and that spark quietly cools. Weeks later they tell me, a little embarrassed, "I still haven't really started."

I'm not telling you that to make you feel bad. I'm telling you because it is the most normal thing in the world, and because this chapter exists to make sure it doesn't happen to you. Everything up to now has been about what AI can do. This chapter is about what you are going to do, this week, with your own two hands. So let me walk you through it the same way I do in the room.

First, Get Your Footing (Secure It Before You Use It)

Before you build anything with AI, take ten minutes to set it up safely. I know, this is not the exciting part. But responsible adoption is what lets you move fast later without looking over your shoulder, and it is the piece most people skip.

Two things to do first. Go into your tool's settings, find where it talks about your data, and turn off the setting that lets your conversations train the model for everyone. You want your information working for you, not quietly feeding the shared pot. Then turn on two-factor authentication, so a password alone can never open your account. That's it. A few minutes of setup, and you can relax and actually use the thing.

Teach It Who You Are

Here is the step that changes everything, and it's the one almost nobody does. Straight out of the box, AI sounds generic, because it doesn't know you yet. Your job is to teach it.

I show this live, and it always gets a reaction. I turn the memory feature off, ask the tool to write something simple like a short blog post, and we read it together. It's fine. It's also flat, the kind of thing that could have been written for anybody. Then I turn memory back on, tell the tool who I am, how I talk, and what I care about, and ask for the same thing again. The second version sounds like a person. It sounds like me. Same tool, same request, night-and-day difference, and the only thing that changed is that it finally knew who it was writing for.

So do that. Turn on memory. Tell your AI your name, your work, your voice, and the way you like things said. Feed it a few things you've already written. The more it knows you, the less generic everything it hands back becomes.

Start in Your Wheelhouse

Now, where to begin. My advice is always the same. Start with the one thing that sits squarely in your wheelhouse, the subject you know cold.

There's a simple reason for that. When you work in an area you know well, you'll catch it the instant AI gets something wrong. You won't be fooled, because you are the expert in the room. That is how you build judgment and trust at the same time. Love photography? Start there. Have a presentation coming up? Open a tool like Gamma and build it. Is there a business you've been meaning to start, a book you've been meaning to write, or a problem that has been sitting on your chest for months? Start there.

And start with something that actually matters to you. Motivation is not a small thing. When the first task is something you care about, you come back to it. When it's a random exercise, you don't. Pick the thing you would be genuinely glad to have finished.

Do This Today

If you close this book and do only one thing, do this. Open your AI tool. Spend ten minutes on the setup we just talked about. Then give it one real task from your own life, something in your wheelhouse that you actually need done. Not a test. A real thing. That single session, one real task carried from start to finish, is the whole on-ramp. Everything after that is just repetition.

When You Get Stuck (And You Will)

Let me name the things that stop people, because knowing them ahead of time takes away half their power.

"I don't have time." You don't need a project. You need one task and fifteen minutes. Start smaller than feels serious.

"It feels like too much." That's almost always because you're staring at all of it at once. Close the other tabs. One tool, one task.

"There are too many tools, I don't know which to pick." Then don't pick a new one. Start with a tool you already have. If you live in Microsoft Word, Copilot is right there. If ChatGPT is already your habit, use that. You do not need a shelf full of tools, you need one, and you almost certainly already own it. My short list of go-to tools is coming right up in the next chapter.

None of these are character flaws. They are just the normal friction of starting something new. Expect them, and walk through them anyway.

From Learner to Doer

Everything in this book comes down to this chapter. Not because the ideas don't matter, they do, but because ideas that never leave the page don't close any gaps. The wealth gap doesn't shrink because we understood AI. It shrinks because we used it, in our businesses, our classrooms, and our communities, and then showed the next person how.

You don't have to be an expert. You don't have to have it all figured out. You just have to open the tool, set it up, and give it one real thing that matters to you. Do that this week. Then do it again next week. That is how a reader becomes a doer, and how a community full of doers starts to change what is possible.

If you don't accept responsibility for your own fate, you'll never get ahead.
~ Regina King

Notes

Chapter 10: Tools for Transformation: AI Resources for Entrepreneurs

As we come to the end of this book, it's impossible not to reflect on the incredible stories that brought this vision to life. At the heart of this journey is my daughter Taylor, who at just twelve years old launched her own business, Taylor's Essence, with the support of artificial intelligence. Her story began with a spark of determination and a three-week deadline, leading her to harness AI to create an impactful, all-natural skincare line. Taylor's journey encapsulates the limitless potential AI offers when combined with passion, creativity, and the courage to try something new.

Taylor's story brings us full circle, showing how the transformative power of AI is not only for established businesses but can also inspire and empower the next generation. As you read this, I hope you feel inspired to harness AI the way Taylor did, using it as a stepping stone to achieve your own goals. Whether you're just starting out, like Taylor, or scaling an established business, like Jennene, the right tools can help turn your vision into reality.

A lot has changed since I first wrote this chapter. Nehemiah told me something in our interview that stuck with me: by his count, there were already over thirty thousand AI tools out there, and that number keeps climbing. That can feel overwhelming if you let it. So instead of trying to chase every new tool, I want to give you a curated list: the ones I keep coming back to, the ones that have proven themselves in Taylor's journey, in my own workshops, and in the stories you've read throughout this book.

Key AI Tools for Entrepreneurs

ChatGPT: A versatile conversational AI, ChatGPT was a central resource in Taylor's journey, helping her develop product recipes, create digital marketing content, and even troubleshoot challenges in production. For entrepreneurs, ChatGPT can serve as an adaptable virtual assistant, handling a variety of tasks from content generation and customer service to strategic brainstorming. Entrepreneurs with limited resources can use ChatGPT as an on-demand team member, increasing productivity and saving time while tackling daily business tasks. (chatgpt.com)

Perplexity: Perplexity is a powerful research tool that enables entrepreneurs to quickly gather and analyze relevant information. Acting as an AI-powered search assistant, Perplexity helps users make informed decisions by simplifying complex data. For entrepreneurs like Taylor who need quick, reliable answers, Perplexity offers instant access to well-sourced information for strategic planning, market research, and competitor analysis. (perplexity.ai)

Gamma: Gamma is an AI tool perfect for creating visually compelling presentations, documents, and reports. Entrepreneurs can use Gamma to create professional pitch decks, business proposals, and project updates that captivate investors, clients, and team members. With Gamma's AI-powered design features, entrepreneurs can turn ideas into presentations quickly, streamlining communication and enhancing engagement. (gamma.app)

Canva: A staple in Taylor's journey, Canva remains one of the most accessible AI-enhanced design platforms. Entrepreneurs use Canva to create everything from logos and social media graphics to marketing materials and product labels. Its intuitive interface and customizable templates make professional design accessible to users of all skill levels. For entrepreneurs who want to build a brand identity without extensive design resources, Canva is an invaluable asset. (canva.com)

Magic School AI: This site offers valuable resources for educators and course creators. It enables interactive lesson planning and personalized learning modules, allowing users to create engaging educational content. For entrepreneurs in learning or skill-building, it provides an efficient way to deliver high-quality, customized experiences. (magicschool.ai)

What's New Since the First Edition

Two years is a long time in AI years. A few tools have earned a permanent place in my own toolkit since I first wrote this chapter, and I want to make sure you have them too.

Microsoft Copilot: If you're already living inside Microsoft 365 (Word, Excel, Outlook, Teams), Copilot meets you right where you are. It's the tool I point people to first when someone tells me they don't have time to learn something new, because it's already sitting inside the software they use every day.

Claude: Built by Anthropic, Claude has become one of the best tools I've found for actually scaling a business. What I love about it is that it takes the lift off your shoulders. Using skills and automation, Claude can carry a task from start to finish while you move on to something else. That's the shift I want you to feel with this new wave of tools: not just getting answers, but actually getting work done.

NotebookLM: This research and organization tool from Google lets you drop in your own documents, whether that's interview transcripts, research reports, or notes from a workshop, and ask questions directly against that material. For entrepreneurs doing their own market research, it's a way to keep your sources straight and cited, not guessed.

AI Agents and Automation: The newest shift in the AI world is what people are calling agentic AI: tools that don't just answer your questions but can go out and complete multi-step tasks on your behalf. We talk about this more in the Leading the Way chapter, but it's worth naming here too. Tools like Zapier and Make are now weaving AI directly into their automations, meaning the busywork of moving information between your systems can increasingly run itself. This is the frontier, and it's worth watching even if you're not ready to adopt it yet.

GoHighLevel (and other all-in-one CRMs): This is one of the questions I get asked most at my workshops: what do I use to actually run my business once I'm past the spreadsheet stage? I use GoHighLevel, and I've found it to be a solid all-in-one system for managing leads, follow-ups, and client communication in one place. It's not the only option out there, there are several strong all-in-one CRMs on the market, but the bigger point is this: if you're still tracking leads and clients in Excel or a Google Sheet, that's the next upgrade to make. A real CRM does the following up for you, so nothing falls through the cracks while you're busy running the business.

Scaling with AI for Economic Empowerment

Taylor's journey with AI shows how even a young entrepreneur can bring an idea to life. But AI's benefits aren't just for beginners; established entrepreneurs also find immense value in these tools. As we learned in Chapter 8, Jennene Biggins, a solopreneur and founder of a text marketing company, leveraged AI to transform her business operations, overcome resource limitations, and scale for growth.

With these AI tools, Jennene achieved a significant productivity boost, increased her client capacity, and, within a month of integrating AI, secured a

$35,000 project. The tools allowed her to operate more efficiently, laying a foundation for financial growth and stability. Her story shows that with the right resources, AI can empower entrepreneurs to overcome obstacles, scale effectively, and achieve long-term economic empowerment.

Empowering the Entrepreneurial Journey with AI

Taylor's and Jennene's stories remind us that AI is not just a tool for productivity; it's a powerful catalyst for economic growth, accessible to anyone with a vision. By incorporating tools like the ones in this chapter, entrepreneurs can overcome limitations, enhance customer relationships, and scale their businesses efficiently. The path to success is no longer restricted by budget, resources, or technical expertise. With AI, anyone, from a young dreamer like Taylor to a seasoned business owner like Jennene, can tap into the transformative power of technology to make their mark.

As you close this chapter, consider how these tools could fit into your own journey. Take inspiration from Taylor's creativity and Jennene's resilience, and use AI to bring your own vision to life. With these resources at your fingertips, the opportunities are endless, and your entrepreneurial dreams are closer than ever before.

"These are the on-ramps in our community. The greatest wealth building opportunity in the history of the planet."
~ Robert F. Smith

Notes

Conclusion: Shaping Our Future with AI

When I sat down to write the first version of this conclusion, I was staring down a deadline, trying to find the right bookend for a book that opened with my daughter Taylor building a skincare business at twelve years old with nothing but a three week deadline and ChatGPT. I wanted the ending to feel as big as that beginning. Looking back, I don't think it quite got there. A lot has happened since then, so I want to try again.

This whole book started with a lightbulb moment, and I don't think I ever said that plainly enough the first time around. I remember the exact feeling of realizing what AI actually was for people who look like the ones I grew up around. It was a genuinely low barrier tool. You didn't need capital. You didn't need a team. You didn't need to already know the right people or have a warm introduction to the right room. For small businesses, for underprivileged communities, for cultures that have historically been locked out of the resources it takes to build wealth, here was something that leveled the field without asking permission first. I could not stop thinking about it. Not long after, I watched my own daughter Taylor prove the whole idea true before I had even finished writing it down.

That instinct wasn't just a feeling, it turns out. Small businesses make up 99.9 percent of all businesses in this country. There are now more than 36 million of them, and together they employ close to half of the entire private sector workforce. In the most recent year on record, small businesses were responsible for about 9 out of every 10 net new jobs created in the whole economy, according to the Small Business Administration. Small business isn't a side story to the American economy. It is the engine. So when I looked at that reality next to what AI could actually do, at a fraction of the cost of hiring a team, the two ideas just clicked into place for me.

Two years ago, when I first wrote about AI, the conversation was mostly about the tools themselves. Learning ChatGPT. Trying Canva. Wondering if this was a fad or the future. Today the conversation has moved. It's not "should I use AI" anymore. It's "how do I get my team using it," "how do I choose from thousands of options," "how do I move from spreadsheets and sticky notes to something that actually runs with me instead of something I have to babysit."

That shift is the whole reason this second edition exists. I told you about Nehemiah's estimate of thirty thousand AI tools back in Chapter 10, and if that number felt overwhelming two years ago, it's almost funny now. But here's what I've learned watching people move through my workshops: the number of tools was never really the problem. The problem was that most people were still treating AI like a search engine, something you ask a question and wait on, instead of what it's actually become, which is a partner. I use Claude the way I used to hope I could use a team member. I hand it something with real substance, using skills and automation, and I go do something else while it works. That's not a small shift. That's the whole shift.

And it's not just individuals feeling that shift. I'm seeing it in the leaders I work with too, the ones trying to bring their teams along instead of leaving them to figure it out alone. Because that's really what closing the wealth gap has always been about in this book. It was never about one person getting ahead. It's about bringing people with you. Every story in these pages, from Myra rebuilding her law practice, to Jennene landing a thirty five thousand dollar project a month after adopting AI, to Taylor at twelve years old, is proof that when someone takes the leap, they don't take it alone. Somebody showed them the door. Now it's your turn to be that person for somebody else.

None of this erases the deeper issue this book started with. The wealth gap in this country didn't happen by accident, and no tool, not even the smartest AI in the world, is going to undo centuries of systemic inequity by itself. AI is neutral. It doesn't care who uses it. That neutrality is exactly why it matters who's in the room when it's built, trained, and deployed. If we're not at that table, bias creeps in, and the gap we're trying to close gets wider instead. So this isn't a hands off kind of hope. It's a hands on one.

Here's what I know for sure, standing where I'm standing after two more years of doing this work in rooms full of real people trying to figure it out. The businesses that grow are the ones that upgrade, not just their tools, but their systems, their teams, and their willingness to hand off the busywork so they can focus on the work that actually matters. I've watched people go from tracking clients in a spreadsheet to running their whole follow up on autopilot, and the look on their face when they realize they didn't lose control, they gained time back, that's the moment I keep chasing every time I step in front of a room.

So let this be the ending I wish I'd written the first time. Taylor is two years older now, and so is every reader who picked up the first edition. Wherever you are in the gap between where you started and where you're headed, AI has gotten a lot better at meeting you there. The tools have changed. The stakes are still the same. Take what's in these pages, pick one thing, and go do it this week. Not someday. This week.

The wealth gap is still here, but so is the opportunity, and it's bigger than it was two years ago. Let's get to work.

"If you're not using AI within the next two years, your businesses and the things you're doing are going to be far behind. You will feel like people are leapfrogging over you if you're not employing this technology."

~ Tonia Bledsoe, AFRO American Newspapers

Acknowledgements

Creating this book would not have been possible without the inspiring stories and contributions of the many entrepreneurs who have used AI to bridge the wealth gap, empower their communities, and open doors for future generations. Each of their journeys provides a beacon of hope and a roadmap for success.

Jennene Biggins: Jennene, founder of Danso Digital Media Group, has transformed her business by integrating AI-driven automation, securing significant projects, and expanding her reach. Her story exemplifies how AI can help solopreneurs scale sustainably, demonstrating the power of determination and the right tools. Learn more about her work at dansodigital mediagroup.com.

Shauna Adams: with The Muse of AI, leverages AI to manage her travel agency's operations and digital presence, showcasing how small businesses can benefit from AI for growth and customer engagement. Her journey is a testament to how AI can simplify daily operations and drive business expansion. Discover her story at themuseofai.com.

Nehemiah Thompson: founder of Start Lean Finish Big, has used AI to automate backend processes and scale his business efficiently. His experience underscores the potential of strategic partnerships and AI to achieve rapid business growth. Explore his approach at startleanfinishbig.com.

Myra Hamilton: As a dedicated attorney, Myra Hamilton integrated AI into her practice to improve client communication and streamline legal services. Her innovations show how AI can support professional services by enhancing productivity and competitiveness. Learn more about her work at hamiltonentertainmentemploymentlawgroup.com and aibizlawyer.com.

Taylor Bledsoe: At just 12 years old, Taylor launched Taylor's Essence with the help of AI, bringing her vision of an all-natural skincare line to life. Her journey is an inspiration to young entrepreneurs, proving that passion and creativity combined with AI can turn dreams into reality. Find her brand at taylorsessence.com.

Alicia Lyttle: has empowered countless individuals by teaching them how to leverage AI and digital skills for business growth and wealth creation. Her work helps demystify AI for entrepreneurs of all backgrounds, fostering a spirit of economic empowerment. Visit her site at alicialyttle.com.

Sonya Hightower-Routt: an educator passionate about technology, has integrated AI into her teaching to equip underserved students with valuable skills. Her dedication to economic empowerment through education highlights the profound impact of AI on bridging opportunity gaps. Learn more about her work at https://thekaleidoschopeproject53.com or https://www.ai4academia.org.

Dr. Jean Hess: A heartfelt thanks also goes to Dr. Jean Hess, who edited the first edition of this book and is the founder of Brainwave Consulting (brainwaveconsulting.com). In addition to being a certified AI consultant, Dr. Jean is a career educator and leader. Her thoughtful guidance and attention to detail helped shape that first edition and gave this book its foundation. Her insights and dedication live on in these pages, even as this second edition has grown well beyond where we started.

Resources: AI-Driven Sales Success: A 5-Step Framework for Amplifying Outbound Strategies

1. **Data Collection and Analysis:** Gather comprehensive customer data. Utilize AI tools to capture and analyze customer interactions across various channels—the result: a detailed understanding of customer behaviors and preferences.

2. **Lead Generation and Prioritization:** Identify and prioritize high-potential leads. Leverage AI algorithms to analyze data and identify leads with the highest probability of conversion. The result: a targeted list of leads for focused outreach.

3. **Personalized Outreach:** Craft tailored messages for effective communication. Use AI-based tools to personalize outreach strategies based on customer data insights. The result: higher engagement rates from personalized communication.

4. **Sales Conversion and Optimization:** Enhance the quality of sales conversations. Implement tools like Gong to analyze sales calls and provide real-time feedback and coaching to sales reps. The result: improved sales techniques and higher success rates in conversations.

5. **Performance Analytics and Continuous Improvement:** Monitor and

enhance sales performance. Regularly review AI-generated analytics to assess sales strategies and identify areas for improvement. The result: continuous refinement of strategies leading to better sales results.